# ARS SALOMONIS

FOUNDATIONS OF PRACTICAL SORCERY VOLUME II

FOUNDATIONS OF PRACTICAL SORCERY VOLUME II

# ARS SALOMONIS

BEING OF THAT HIDDEN ARTE OF SOLOMON THE KING

## Gary St. M. Nottingham

Published by Avalonia
www.avaloniabooks.co.uk

*Published by Avalonia*

BM Avalonia
London
WC1N 3XX
England, UK
www.avaloniabooks.co.uk

**ARS SALOMONIS**
Copyright G. St. M. Nottingham Midsummer Eve 2011

First Edition 2012.
This revised edition, 2015.

All rights reserved.

ISBN 978-1-905297-75-7

Design by Satori, for Avalonia.

British Library Cataloguing in Publication Data. A catalogue record for this book is available from the British Library.

All rights reserved. No part of this publication may be reproduced or utilised in any form or by any means, electronic or mechanical, including photocopying, microfilm, recording, or by any information storage and retrieval system, or used in another book, without written permission from the author.

## *About the Author*

**Gary St. M. Nottingham's** commitment to the study and practice of the alchemical arte, ritual magic, grimoires and spirit conjuration means that he can often be found peering at bubbling flasks or a shewstone – or otherwise engaged in deepening his knowledge and understanding of such matters. His practices also draw on the work of the 17th-century astrologer William Lilly and the arte of horary astrology.

Gary was raised in south Shropshire, where, during his mid-teens, he became involved with a small Coven, thereby gaining an excellent grounding in a wide selection of magical practices. Following the conjuration of a spirit, and asking it for help that manifested when least expected, he subsequently became involved with a group of practising alchemists. He has a background in horticulture, enjoys spending time in the garden and playing chess. He organised the legendary Ludlow Esoteric Conference (2004-2008), helped produce *Verdelet* occult magazine, has taught many free day workshops on basic occult skills and is a popular speaker at esoteric conferences.

The seven volumes of *Foundations of Practical Sorcery* are an unabridged collection of Gary's much sought-after previously published work, updated and made available to a wider readership at last.

# Table of Contents

INTRODUCTION ............................................................................................. 8

OF OUR ARTE ............................................................................................... 11
O CREATURE OF TALISMAN ...................................................................... 16
MODUS OPERANDI ..................................................................................... 67
NON NOBIS DOMINI ................................................................................... 71

INDEX ............................................................................................................ 88

# Introduction

We live in an age where we are awash with information on all subjects, and to this the magical artes are no exception. Whilst the student of magic can easily access all manner of electronic files there is nothing quite like a book.

A book can not only be picked up and read, but will, in many instances, over time, become a friend, guide and teacher who has assisted the reader on their journey throughout their life. Quite simply books can change lives and this is why those who have been in positions of power through the centuries have tried, and often failed, to keep knowledge out of the hands of everyday folk. This is perhaps primarily because they feared the power of the book to cause change, and change is what the seven books in the Foundations of Practical Sorcery series will cause.

Today the magical artes have never been so accessible, although that doesn't mean the demands that the arte makes upon the practitioner have been lessened in any way. While the arte is, in principle, for all, not everyone will have the self-discipline, the will and the imagination to succeed therein. However for those who do have these basic attributes or are prepared to acquire them there is much to be gained from the practice of magic in all levels of life. For many people their ingress into the arte will be by books, and the exploration of and working with the information they contain. There is nothing like experience even if your magic proves less successful than hoped for: there is no such thing as failure in magic, because every experience will, at the very least, teach the practitioner something, even if it's just to try harder next time!

Of course some will have access to a magical group and the knowledge and collective experience to be found therein; but for many this will not be the case. Magical groups regardless of hue by and large have much to commend them, but not all of them do. I have in the past been approached by people who have gone through a coven system yet then been led to ask me to help them practice and study magic. It seemed their coven did not in fact practice the arte; which left me wondering what was it that they did do. I am aware of similar approaches made to other magical practitioners, which has left me concluding that some magical groups and covens can actually be detrimental to an individual's magical development and understanding - although this is certainly not the case with all by any means.

Foundations of Practical Sorcery goes some way to rectifying this deficit in any student's magical life. They offer clear magical instruction and accounts of magical acts to be performed, thus making the arte easily accessible. The methods and techniques presented are all based upon my own personal knowledge and experience which goes back over forty years, methods and techniques that have worked successfully for me and will do so for any reader who applies them accordingly.

In many ways I was fortunate, during the autumn of 1972, to meet a magical practitioner who taught me much regarding the arte, generously affording me the run of their magical library as well. Having been schooled extensively in magical knowledge from my mid teen years I consider myself to have been extremely fortunate and lucky to have had many experiences not easily available to many people. Thus the present Foundations of Practical Sorcery series is the distillation of four decades of successful magical workings.

Each of the seven volumes gives a clear account and rendition of one or another area of magical instruction that I have received and have been taught. They are presented to the reader in a clear and workable style which will provide them with a concise and firm foundation, allowing the serious magical student to explore the Western Magical Tradition, the inheritance of us all.

*Gary St. M. Nottingham, February 2015*

CHAPTER ONE

# Of Our Arte

> '*O My Son Roboam…..of all sciences there is none more useful than the knowledge of celestial movements.*'

Whilst the *Key of Solomon* is by tradition attributed to the biblical king of that name, there is as far as I am aware no evidence that he was responsible for the work. Although the *'Key'* of all of the grimoire traditions is perhaps the most widely known, it has not been until modern times published in its entirety. There are several variant manuscripts which claim to be part of the *'Solomonic Family'* and most have in recent times been published by the eminent occult scholars David Rankine, Stephen Skinner and Joseph Peterson. But it is the work of Samuel Liddell MacGregor Mathers, and in particular his version of the *Pentacles of Solomon*, that I wish to consider. In 1888 George Redway first published Mather's version of the *'Key'* and until recently it was the definitive version, and it is the Pentacles therein with which this work is concerned. Mathers, who spent his days in the reading room of the British Museum studying occult manuscripts, was described by W. B. Yeats thus,

> '*At the British Museum Reading Room I often saw a man of thirty-six or thirty-seven, in a brown velveteen coat, with a gaunt resolute face and an athletic body, who seemed before I heard his name or knew the nature of his studies, a figure of romance. He had copied many manuscripts on ceremonial magic in the British Museum and many more continental libraries.*'

Mathers informs the reader in his version of the *'Key'* that,

> '*I see no reason to doubt the tradition which assigns the authorship of the Key to King Solomon, for among others Josephus the Jewish historian mentions the magical works attributed to that monarch. This is confirmed by many Eastern traditions and his magical skill is frequently mentioned in the*

*Arabian Nights.'*

Granted that absence of evidence is not evidence of absence, Mather's view on the antiquity of the *'Key'* cannot be considered as proof. However the opinion of Rankine and Skinner, with their comments in their work *The Veritable Key of Solomon*, where they suggest that the *'Key'* is of Greek origin, may very well be right. But what is certain is that the *'Key'*, which had been a collection of manuscripts, until Mathers gave then some order, is old. Mathers tells us that the Hebrew characters around the pentacles were badly drawn for which he blames past scribes for their lack of care and understanding.

However he managed, with the help of Dr Wynn Westcott, to reconstruct them, something which was no small task. The first hint of antiquity is given by Josephus in the first century CE when he mentions that a book exists with incantations for the summoning of demons which is associated with Solomon; he recalls how a Jew named Eleazar used it to cure cases of possession. Accounts appear in the eleventh century with Psellus referring to a treatise on stones and demons composed by Solomon.

During the year 1350, on the orders of Pope Innocent Sixth, *Le Livre de Salomon*, a work which gave details on spirit evocation, was burnt and declared heretical. And in 1456 Hartlieb declares to Duke John of Burgundy that *Sigilum Salomonis* and the *Clavicula Salomonis* were highly regarded works and it was no doubt from these and other manuscripts that the *'Key,'* was created. It contains no Christian elements but it clearly demonstrates a familiarity with Kabbalistic concepts which suggests a Jewish origin, as does the liberal use of *Psalms*. From the instructions given I would suggest that it is assumed that the operator is conversant with magical praxis, however I have made the assumption that not all readers of this work will be so able and have therefore given a modus operandi where relevant. But I would urge a good grounding in Kabbalistic cosmology, meditation and symbolism as the Kabbalah is the bedrock of the *'Key.'* Therefore an ongoing programme of meditation, study and astral exploration of the Tree of Life will prove to be invaluable to the student of the *'Key.'*

Thus the mysteries of the Kabbalah and the potencies of its symbolism will become part of the warp and weft of the soul and will in time promote those indispensable occult virtues of concentration, visualisation and willpower without which your magic will not come to birth; as all magic must firstly happen on the subtle levels before manifesting in the mundane world. With the rise of the Hermetic Order of the Golden Dawn in late Victorian England, which Mathers was the primary, but not the only driving force behind, a different approach to magic than had been previously practiced before was developed. Looking at the grimoire traditions and the operations of the arte, as laid down by Francis Barrett in *The Magus,* the approach to magic was based very much on purity by long fasts, chastity, the use of *Psalms* and prayers to God and self-abasement. The Golden Dawn approach was different. Whilst abstinence and a period of withdrawal were seen as useful aids to concentrate the magical will, the magical modus of Samuel Liddell MacGregor Mathers was to exalt the magical will and by dint of one's own divinity the magic was brought to birth.

Hence the use of God Names with a descending hierarchy of angelic beings whose aid was invoked for success in the operation of the arte … *'as I do will, So Mote It Be.'* This approach, coupled with fasts and prayers, will invariably bring the magical success desired. Although the *'Key'* gives accounts of the consecration of the *'tools of the arte'* with the use of *Psalms* and prayers this method is not the only means of consecration that can be employed. But however you proceed; consecrated and dedicated tools of the arte will be needed.

As indeed is a secure place that is free from disturbance whilst the operation is being performed and don't forget to turn off the phone. Solomon's approach to the arte is one of conjuration and the spirits concerned with the talismans within the *'Key'* are to be summoned by long and potent invocations to consecrate the seals and attend to one's will. The method presented here is twofold: firstly a less complex system of consecration via the Middle Pillar exercise, adapted for this work, and secondly by conjuration into the shewstone of the spirits, for the consecration of the talisman; this latter method is somewhat more demanding. Whilst the *'Key'* instructs that the proper time for the performing of these operations of the arte is to be within their planetary hours, this is not the only means of timing; as astrological configurations can be considered as an alternative. For example, planetary hours are worked out by calculating the amount of time between sunrise and sunset (consult with an ephemeris) and dividing the time by twelve to give you the number of minutes in a planetary hour for the day.

This will differ at various times of the year as days are longer in the summer months then the winter. If you have an understanding of astrology which all students of the arte who are worth their salt will have, then cast an astrological chart to see when the planet that you are working with is in the first or tenth house where it will be at its most potent, more so if not hindered by any malefic. However Solomon makes it quite clear that:-

> *The days and hours of Saturn are useful….. to summon the souls of the dead, but only those who have died a natural death. To create good or bad fortune to buildings; to have familiar spirits; for good or ill to a business, possessions, goods, seeds, fruit or similar. The acquiring of learning, to bring destruction and death also to sow hatred and discord.*
> *The days and hours of Jupiter will grant honour, riches, friendships, good luck and the preservation of health.*
> *In the days and hours of Mars one can create strife and war; to gain military honour, acquire courage and to overthrow enemies.*
> *The days and hours of the Sun grant wealth, gain, the favour of people great and small, good health, divination and to make peace.*
> *With the days and hours of Venus one can create love and friendships, joyous and pleasant undertakings and also good luck.*
> *The days and hours of Mercury will provide eloquence, intelligence, success in business ventures and travel also all communications. However it also governs theft and deceit.*
> *Whilst the days and hours of the Moon grant success in divination, domestic matters, womanhood, births, children and travel particularly by water.*

Furthermore consider a waxing moon for matters of a constructive nature and a waning moon for those of a malefic or destructive concern. Solomon instructs that the working place needs to be away from those who are foolish, vain and stupid, and also away from the habitation of men; and that the best place to work is somewhere that is desolate and quiet ideally at a crossroads at night time, although this may very well be impracticable. If all else fails then a quiet room that has been consecrated and blessed will suffice. A magical circle needs to be inscribed and consecrated for the work. Solomon gives a clear design with the names of God inscribed there around; an alternative would be to use the God Names and Archangelic names appertaining unto the work.

## The Planetary Hours

| Sun. | Mon. | Tues. | Wed. | Hours from Sunset to Sunset | Hours from Midnight to Midnight | Thurs. | Fri. | Sat. |
|---|---|---|---|---|---|---|---|---|
| Merc. | Jup. | Ven. | Sat. | 8 | 1 | Sun. | Moon. | Mars. |
| Moon. | Mars. | Mer. | Jup. | 9 | 2 | Ven. | Sat. | Sun. |
| Sat. | Sun. | Moon. | Mars. | 10 | 3 | Mer. | Jup. | Ven. |
| Jup. | Ven. | Sat. | Sun | 11 | 4 | Moon. | Mars. | Mer. |
| Mars. | Mer. | Jup. | Ven. | 12 | 5 | Sat. | Sun. | Moon. |
| Sun. | Moon. | Mars | Mer. | 1 | 6 | Jup. | Ven. | Sat. |
| Ven. | Sat. | Sun. | Moon. | 2 | 7 | Mars. | Mer. | Jup. |
| Mer. | Jup. | Ven. | Sat. | 3 | 8 | Sun. | Moon. | Mars. |
| Moon. | Mars. | Mer. | Jup. | 4 | 9 | Ven. | Sat. | Sun. |
| Sat. | Sun. | Moon. | Mars. | 5 | 10 | Mer. | Jup. | Ven. |
| Jup. | Ven. | Sat. | Sun. | 6 | 11 | Moon. | Mars. | Mer. |
| Mars. | Mer. | Jup. | Ven. | 7 | 12 | Sat. | Sun. | Moon. |
| Sun. | Moon. | Mars. | Mer. | 8 | 1 | Jup. | Ven. | Sat. |
| Ven. | Sat. | Sun. | Moon. | 9 | 2 | Mars. | Mer. | Jup. |
| Mer. | Jup. | Ven. | Sat. | 10 | 3 | Sun. | Moon. | Mars. |
| Moon. | Mars. | Mer. | Jup. | 11 | 4 | Ven. | Sat. | Sun. |
| Sat. | Sun. | Moon. | Mars. | 12 | 5 | Mer. | Jup. | Ven. |
| Jup. | Ven. | Sat. | Sun. | 1 | 6 | Moon. | Mars. | Mer. |
| Mars. | Mer. | Jup. | Ven. | 2 | 7 | Sat. | Sun. | Moon. |
| Sun. | Moon. | Mars. | Mer. | 3 | 8 | Jup. | Ven. | Sat. |
| Ven. | Sat. | Sun. | Moon. | 4 | 9 | Mars. | Mer. | Jup. |
| Mer. | Jup. | Ven. | Sat. | 5 | 10 | Sun. | Moon. | Mars. |
| Moon. | Mars. | Mer. | Jup. | 6 | 11 | Ven. | Sat. | Sun. |
| Sat. | Sun. | Moon. | Mars. | 7 | 12 | Mer. | Jup. | Ven. |

CHAPTER TWO

# O Creature of Talisman

> *'If thou invokes these spirits By the virtue of these pentacles They will obey thee without repugnance.'*

As Solomon tells us, these pentacles which are made will not only bring the spirits to obedience but will also have *'wonderful and excellent virtue.'* And furthermore they are of use against all perils of the Earth, Air, Water and Fire. They are also effective against binding, sortilege, sorcery and against all terror and fear wherever thou shalt find thyself. If armed with them thou shalt be in safety all the days of thy life. Through them do we acquire grace and good will from mankind and that all things are obedient to the names of God therein. Size is not of importance with these pentacles, although obviously they will need to be big enough to see what they are, it is important that they are made from virgin material; that is something that has not been used before for anything else. Solomon also advises not to abuse the arte herein but also to share it with those who are worthy of it and can appreciate it.

> *'…never must thou lavish these things among the ignorant, for that would be as blameable as to cast precious gems before swine; on the contrary, from one sage the secret knowledge should pass unto another sage, for in this manner shall the treasure of treasures never descend into oblivion.'*

## THE FIRST PENTACLE OF SATURN

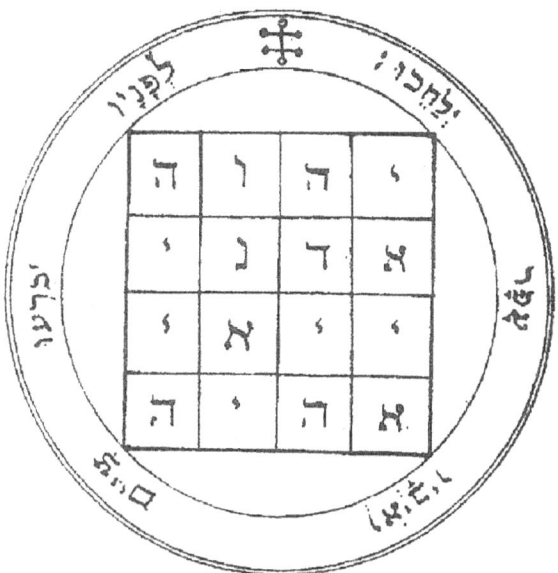

God Name for all of the saturnine pentacles is: YHVH ELOHIM meaning *Lord God*

Archangel: Tzaphkiel meaning *Beholder of God*

The spirits are of the order of the Aralim

Colour: Black

Incense: Myrrh

This is of great use and value for striking terror in the spirits. Wherefore upon it being shown to them they submit and kneeling upon the earth before it they obey.

Around the square are the four Great Names of God which are written with the four letters IHVH. YOD HEH VAU HEH; ADNI. ADONIA; IIAI, YIAI (has the same numerical value as EL and can therefore be used as such): AHIH, EHIEH:

The Hebrew vesicle around is *Psalm* 72:9

> 'The Ethiopians shall kneel before him, His enemies shall lick dust.'

**THE SECOND PENTACLE OF SATURN**

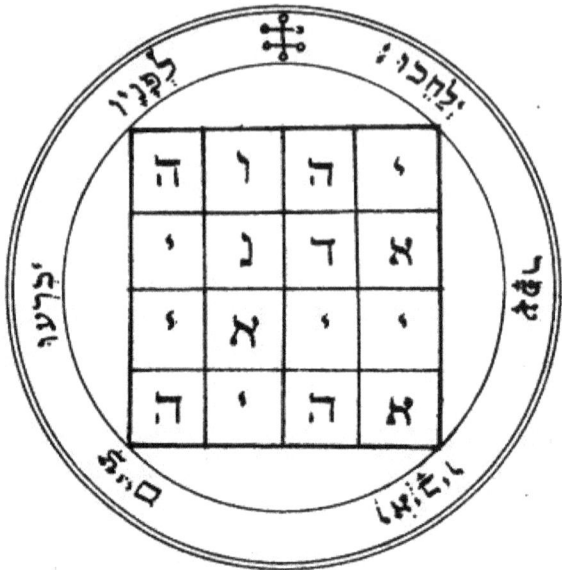

The second pentacle of Saturn is of great value against adversity and is of use in repressing the pride of the spirits. The Hebrew lettering in the square is the celebrated Sator square which can be dated back to the 2nd century CE and has been continually used in magic ever since.

SATOR AREPO TENET OPERA ROTAS

The words can be read from either side or up and down this was considered to be a square of great magical power in medieval times. However the Hebrew in the squares is written from left to right when in practice it is written from right to left. The Hebrew vesicle surrounding the pentacle is from Psalm 72:8

> …'his dominion shall be also from the one sea to the other, and from the flood unto the worlds end.'

## THE THIRD PENTACLE OF SATURN

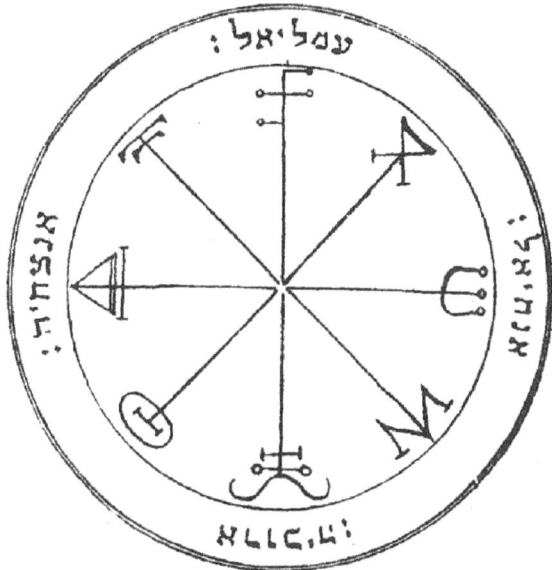

The third pentacle of Saturn should be made within the magical circle and is good to be used at night when the spirits of Saturn are invoked. The figures at the end of the arms within the charm are figures associated with Saturn. Going deosil that is with the sun the Hebrew characters are the names of four saturnine spirits Omeliel, Anachiel, Arauchiah and Anazachia. These spirits being of Saturn will work within the office of the planet and will produce results according to the planet's nature.

Omeliel                     Anachiel

Arauchiah                   Anazachia

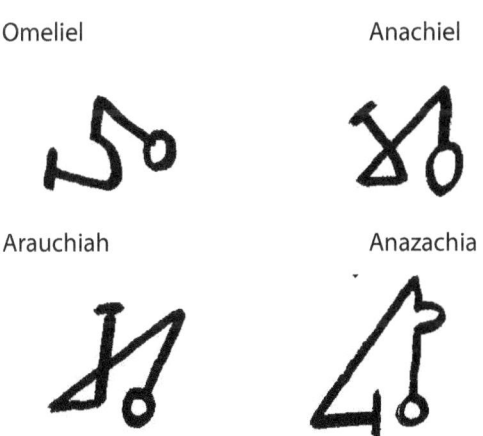

## THE FOURTH PENTACLE OF SATURN

The fourth pentacle of Saturn will produce destruction and ruin. It will also invoke those spirits from the south who will bring news of a particular event or person if invoked from that side. The Hebrew around the triangle reading from top left side is from *Deut* 4:6 and reads:

'..Hear O Israel, IHVH ALHINV is IHVH ACHD.'

The surrounding vesicle is from *Deut* 109:18

'As he clothed himself with cursing like as with a garment so let it come into his bowels like water and like oil into his bones.'

The centre of the triangle contains the letter YOD.

**THE FIFTH PENTACLE OF SATURN**

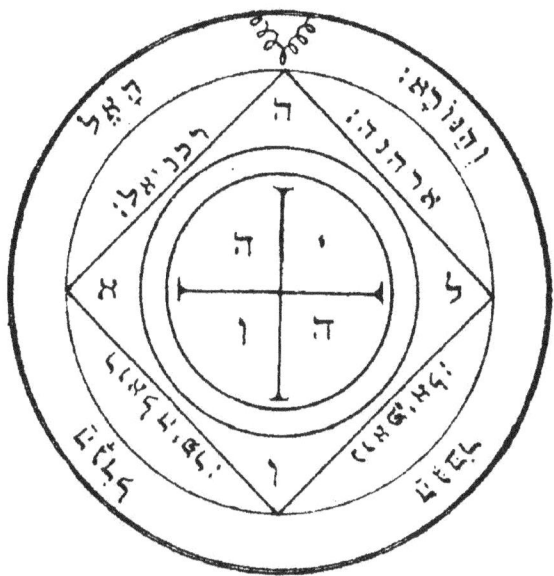

The fifth pentacle of Saturn defends against the spirits of Saturn when thou invokest them at night and will chase away those spirits who guard treasure. The Hebrew letters in the angles of the cross are those of the name IHVH. The letters in the square form the word ALVH…ELOAH. Around the four sides of the square are the names of the angels Arehanah, Rakhaniel, Roelhaiphar and Noaphiel.

The vesicle around the pentacle is from *Deut* 10:17

'…*A Great God, a Mighty and Terrible..*'

Arehanah     Rakhaniel

Roelhaiphar     Noaphiel

**THE SIXTH PENTACLE OF SATURN**

The sixth pentacle contains various symbols associated with Saturn. If it is pronounced against a person they will be obsessed by demons and madness.

Around the periphery is written in Hebrew letters:

> 'Set thou a wicked one to be ruler over him and let Satan stand at his right hand.'

## THE SEVENTH PENTACLE OF SATURN

The last pentacle of Saturn excites earthquakes seeing that the power of each order of Angels herein invoked is sufficient to make the whole Universe tremble. The pentacle contains written therein the nine orders of angels:

Chaioth Ha–Qadesch - Holy Living Creatures, Auphanim – Wheels, Aralim – Thrones, Chashmalim -Brilliant Ones, Seraphim – Fiery, Malakim – Kings, Elohim – Gods, Beni Elohim - Sons of Gods, Kerubim - Strong Ones

The vesicle is from *Psalm* 18:7

> '..Then the earth shook and trembled. The foundation of the hills also moved and were shaken because he was wroth.'

## THE FIRST PENTACLE OF JUPITER

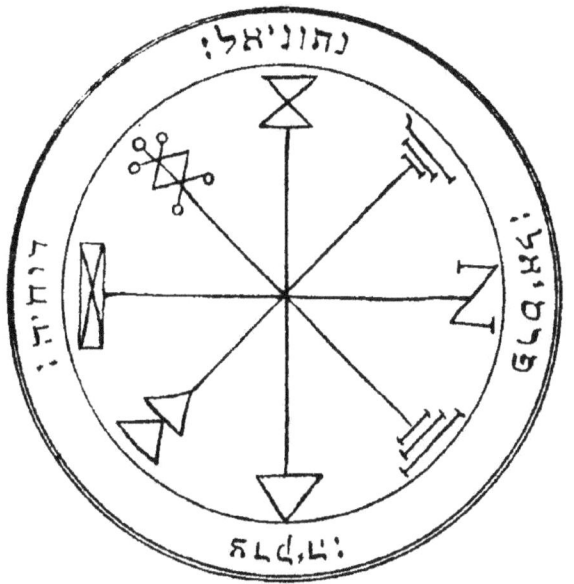

God name for all the Jupiter talismans is El meaning *God*

Archangel Tzadkiel meaning *Righteous of God*

Order of Angels Chashmalim

Colour Blue

Incense Cedar

The first pentacle of Jupiter serves to invoke the spirits of Jupiter, particularly those whose names are written here around. Its lord is Parasiel who teaches how to acquire treasure. Whilst this pentacle has the symbols of Jupiter around on the eight arms, the top left symbol is the planetary seal of Saturn and it should be that of Jupiter. Perhaps a scribe's error? The names of the angels around the perimeter are Netonial, Davachiah, Tzedeqiah and Parasiel, whose sigils are these below.

Netonial

Davachiah

Tzedeqiah

Parasiel

## THE SECOND PENTACLE OF JUPITER

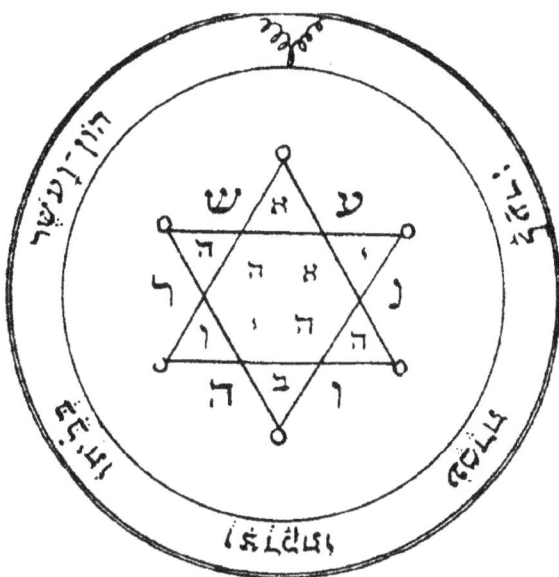

With this second pentacle of Jupiter can be acquired glory, honour, riches and all good things. Together with great tranquillity of mind. In the centre of the Hexagram are the letters of the name AHIH EHIEH. In the upper and lower angles of the hexagram is the name AB father and in the remaining angles is the name IHVH.

The vesicle around is from *Psalm* 112:3

> '..wealth and riches are in his house and his righteousness endureth forever.'

## THE THIRD PENTACLE OF JUPITER

The third pentacle of Jupiter protects those who evoke the spirits of Jupiter to which they are obedient. In the top left corner is the seal of Jupiter which as I pointed out earlier should be on the first pentacle instead of the seal of Saturn. Within it is the name IHVH. In the top right corner is ADNI Adoni. Below in the bottom right quarter is IHVH, YOD – HEH – VAU – HEH. In the bottom left corner is the seal of the planetary intelligence for Jupiter Yophiel.

Around the edge is a verse from *Psalm* 125:1

> '..They that trust in IHVH shall be as Mount Zion which cannot be removed but abideth forever.'

## THE FOURTH PENTACLE OF JUPITER

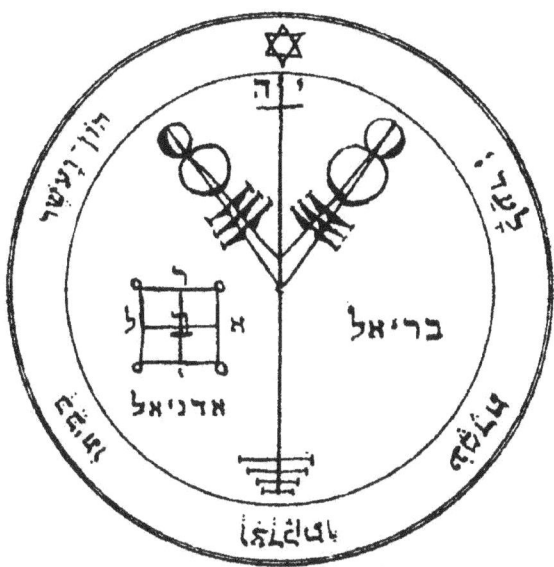

The fourth pentacle of Jupiter serves to grant riches and honour. Its angel is Bariel. The pentacle should be engraved upon silver in the day and hour of Jupiter when the planet is in the sign of Cancer. At the top of the seal are the two angels associated with this pentacle, Adoniel and Bariel is on the right side of the talisman.

The vesicle is from *Psalm* 112:3

> '..wealth and riches are in his house and his righteousness endureth for ever.'

Adoniel                    Bariel

## THE FIFTH PENTACLE OF JUPITER

The fifth pentacle has great power and will promote visions. The letters within the pentacle are all taken from the last word around the talisman, whilst Mathers informs us that they have a mystical meaning to them he says no more about them.

The vesicle around is taken from the book of *Ezekiel* 1:1.

> '..as I was among the captives of Chebar the heavens were opened and I saw visions of Elohim.'

## THE SIXTH PENTACLE OF JUPITER

This sixth pentacle of Jupiter serves to protect against all earthly danger. The talisman must be devoutly regarded each day with the vesicle around it being recited.

The four names within the cross are the names of the elemental rulers. Starting from the top and going sunwise are the following:-

Seraph (fire) – Tharsis (water) – Ariel (earth) – Cherub (air)

The vesicle is from *Psalm* 22:16-17

> '..they pierced my hands and my feet, I may tell all my bones.'

## THE SEVENTH PENTACLE OF JUPITER

The last pentacle of Jupiter is considered to have great power against poverty when the vesicle that surrounds it is recited with devotion. The talisman helps to acquire treasure.

On the arms of the wheel are the mystical characters of Jupiter.

The verse that surrounds the talisman is from *Psalm* 113:7

> '..lifting the poor out of the mire and raising the needy from the dung hill
> that he may set him with princes even with the princes of his people.'

## THE FIRST PENTACLE OF MARS

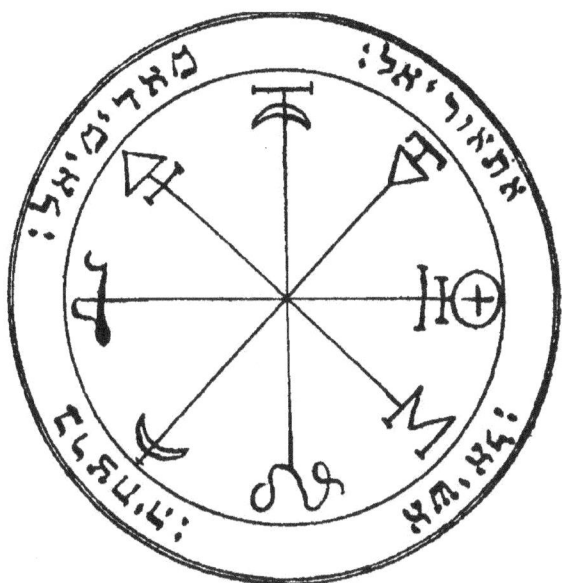

God Name for all the talismans of Mars ELOHIM GIBOR meaning *God of Battles*

Archangel Khamael, *The Burner of God*

Order of Angels Seraphim, *The Fiery Serpents*

Colour Red

Incense Dragon's Blood

The first pentacle of Mars is for invoking the spirits of Mars particularly those whose names are written there around. The sigils on the seal are signs belonging to the nature of Mars, and around the talisman are the names of the four angels of Mars. Top left Madimiel, this is a derivative of the Hebrew word Madim meaning Mars. The second name bottom left is Bartzachiah from the Mars spirit Bartzabel. The third name bottom right is Eschiel and the fourth name is Ithuriel.

Madimiel

Bartzachiah

Eschiel

Ithuriel

## THE SECOND PENTACLE OF MARS

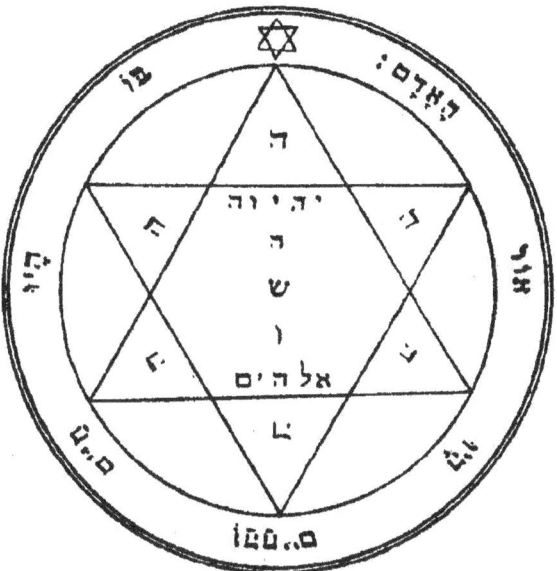

The second pentacle of Mars serves with success against disease if applied to the afflicted parts.

The five letters descending within the hexagram are IHShVH or YOD-HEH-SHIN-VAV-HEH. These letters traditionally represent the four elements plus spirit and form the name Yesheshuah the name which has become Jesus. Thus man made holy by the descent of the spirit.

The vesicle around the talisman is from *John* 1:4.

   *'In him was the life and the life was the light of man.'*

## THE THIRD PENTACLE OF MARS

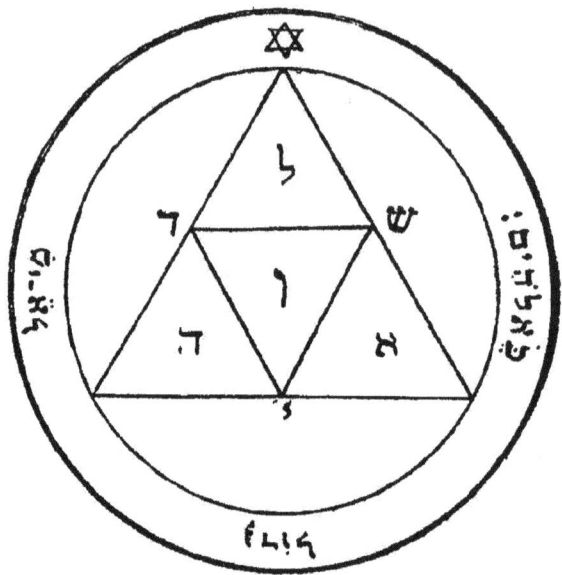

The third pentacle of Mars is potent in causing war, wrath and discord. It will also resist enemies and will quell rebellious spirits.

In the centre is the letter VAU and the vesicle around is from *Psalm* 77:13.

*'..who is so Great a God as our Elohim.'*

## THE FOURTH PENTACLE OF MARS

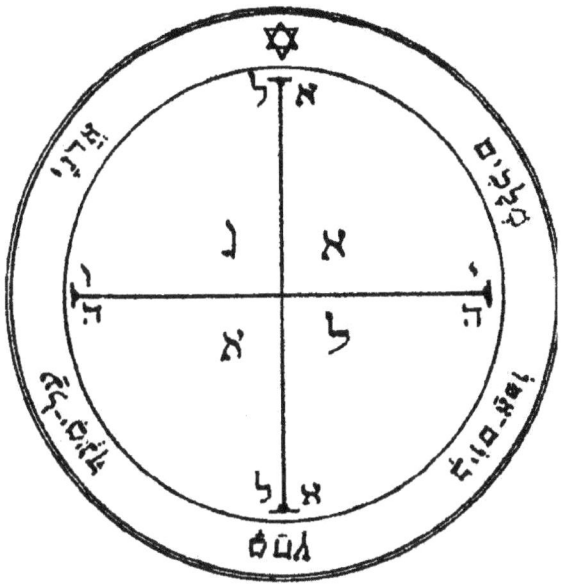

The fourth pentacle of Mars will grant victory in wars, disputes and struggles.

In the centre is the Kabbalistic name AGLA.

On the right and left arms of the cross are the letters YOD-HEH-VAV-HEH. At the top and at the bottom are the letters EL.

The verse around the periphery is from *Psalm* 110:5

*'..the Lord at thy right hand
shall wound even kings in the day of his wrath.'*

## THE FIFTH PENTACLE OF MARS

The fifth pentacle of Mars is to be written on virgin parchment and is terrible unto demons and at the sight of it they will obey thee.

The vesicle is from *Psalm* 91:13.

> '..thou shalt go upon the lion and adder, the young lion and the dragon
> shalt thou tread under thy feet.'

## THE SIXTH PENTACLE OF MARS

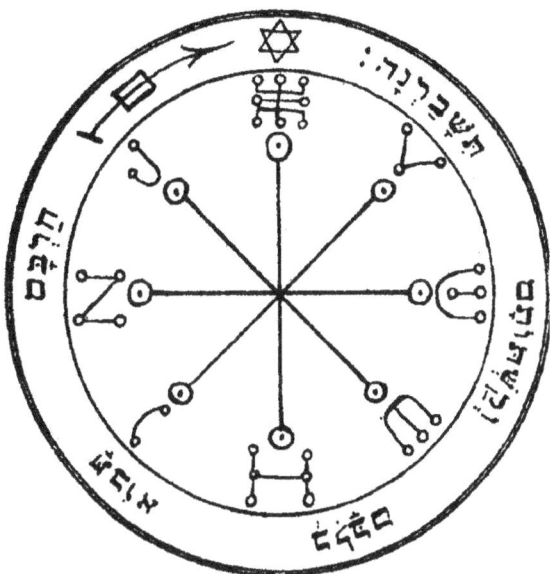

The sixth pentacle of Mars has so great a virtue that being armed therewith, if attacked you will not be injured or wounded when fighting. It is a pentacle of protection.

Around the arms of the central wheel, and written in the Malachi alphabet, are the words,

'Elohim Qeber, Elohim hath protected.'

The vesicle surrounding the pentacle is from *Psalm* 37:15

'..their sword shall enter into their own heart and their bow shall be broken.'

## THE SEVENTH PENTACLE OF MARS

This last pentacle of Mars has the power to produce rains and storms if it is drawn on virgin parchment. The spirits there around, these names are written in the Celestial script, which is a magical variant of the Hebrew alphabet.

In the centre of the pentacle are the divine names EL and YIAI which have the same numerical value.

The vesicle that is around the talisman is taken from *Psalm* 105:32-33

> '..he gave them hail for rain and flaming fire in their land.
> He smote their vines also their fig trees.'

## THE FIRST PENTACLE OF THE SUN

God Name for all talismans of the Sun: YHVH ALOAH VA DAATH meaning *God made manifest in the sphere of the mind*

Archangel: Mikael meaning *The Perfect of God*

Order of Angels: Malakim

Colour: Gold

Incense: Frankincense

The first pentacle of the Sun. The countenance of Shaddai the Almighty whose aspect all creatures obey and the angelic spirits do reverence. All spirits are subject unto this talisman as it contains the figure of Metatron the Archangel of Kether, who is referred to as vice-regent the Archangel nearest to God.

In the middle of the pentacle on either side of the head is written EL SHADDAI.

Around the periphery is written in Latin

> 'Behold his face and form By whom all things were made And whom all creatures obey.'

## THE SECOND PENTACLE OF THE SUN

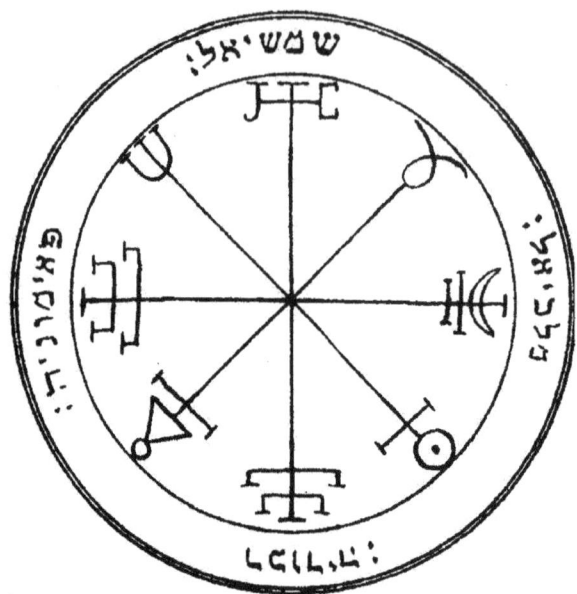

This, the second pentacle of the Sun, will help to control the solar spirits who are prideful and arrogant.

The four angels who are associated with this pentacle are:

Shemeshiel    Paimoniah

Rekhodiah    Malkhiel

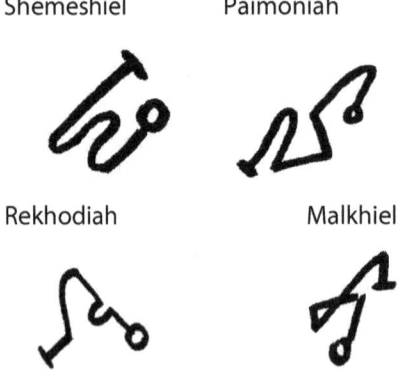

## THE THIRD PENTACLE OF THE SUN

The third pentacle of the Sun serves to acquire renown, glory and material wealth; it will also inflict loss. YHVH the Tetragrammaton is written twelve times therein. Although it is a character from a magical script called angelic writing, the figure at the top of the talisman with eight arms and stations perhaps equates with the eight stations of the Sun as it travels through the year. But as a letter it represents the Hebrew letter samekh. This equates with the twenty-fifth Kabbalistic path from Yesod – Luna, to Tiphereth –Sun, which can be seen as imagery to invoke and work with the energies thereof.

The vesicle around the edge is from the book of *Daniel* 4:34

> *'My kingdom is an everlasting kingdom and my domain endureth from age to age.'*

**THE FOURTH PENTACLE OF THE SUN**

The fourth pentacle of the Sun will enable you to see the spirits as it compels them to appear visible when they are evoked and the pentacle is uncovered.

In the centre is written the names IHVH and also ADONAI, whilst around the arms of the talisman are written characters from the magical script *'Passing of the River.'* The letters from the top going around widdershins (anticlockwise) are, YOD - HEH - VAU - HEH - ALEPH - DALETH - NUN - YOD - YHVH - ADNI. This is also spelt out at the centre of the wheel.

The vesicle around the edge is from *Psalm* 13:3-4

> *'Lighten mine eyes that I sleep not in death, Lest mine enemy say I have prevailed against him.'*

**THE FIFTH PENTACLE OF THE SUN**

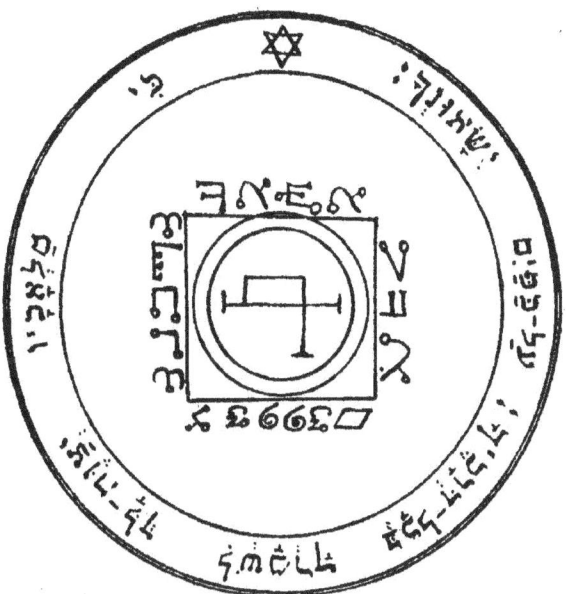

This the fifth pentacle of the Sun will help with long journeys as its spirits are useful in creating trouble-free travel.

The characters around the square that is in the middle of the talisman are from the script previously mentioned, *'Passing of the River.'* They spell in Hebrew the names of the angels that are associated with the talismanic figure which are

samekh - heh- samekh - daleth – resh – yod – beth – cheth – resh – peh – lamed –peh – peh- lamed – mem – aleph – daleth – nun

The vesicle is from *Psalm* 91:11-12

> 'He shall give his angels charge over thee To keep thee in all thy ways
> They shall bear thee up in their hands.'

## THE SIXTH PENTACLE OF THE SUN

The sixth pentacle of the Sun serves for all operations of invisibility and concealment when correctly made. Mathers says that the central figure within the circle that is in the triangle is the letter YOD from the *'Passing of the River'* script. He is wrong as this is the letter Qoph.

The three characters, again in the same script, that appear in the angles of the triangle are SHIN DALETH YOD or SHADDAI.

The vesicle surrounding is from *Psalm* 69:23 and from *Psalm* 135:16.

> *'Let their eyes be darkened that they see not And make their loins to continually shake.*
> *They have eyes and they see not.'*

## THE SEVENTH PENTACLE OF THE SUN

The last pentacle of the Sun, if engraved on gold on the day and in the hour of the Sun, is of use to set free those who are imprisoned or detained against their will.

In the arms of the cross and starting with the top and working widdershins are the names of the four angels of the elements.

Chasan – air          Ariel – fire

Phorlakh – earth  Taliahad – water

Between the arms of the cross are the names of the rulers of each element. Ariel – Seraph – Tharsis – Cherub. The vesicle around is from *Psalm* 116:16–17

> *'Thou hast broken my bonds in sunder.*
> *I will offer unto thee the sacrifice of thanksgiving and I will call upon the name IHVH.'*

## THE FIRST PENTACLE OF VENUS

God Name for all Venusian talismans: YHVH Tzaboath meaning *Lord of Hosts/Armies*.

Archangel: Haniel meaning *I, the God*

Order of Angels: Elohim

Colour: Green

Incense: Rose

The first pentacle of Venus is for the invocation of Venusian spirits. More so for those whose names are written here around and who perform the offices of Venus. The angels are Nogahiel (from the Hebrew word for Venus – Nogah), Acheliah, Socohiah, and Nangariel.

The seals of the angels are

Nogahiel

Acheliah

Socohiah

Nangariel

## THE SECOND PENTACLE OF VENUS

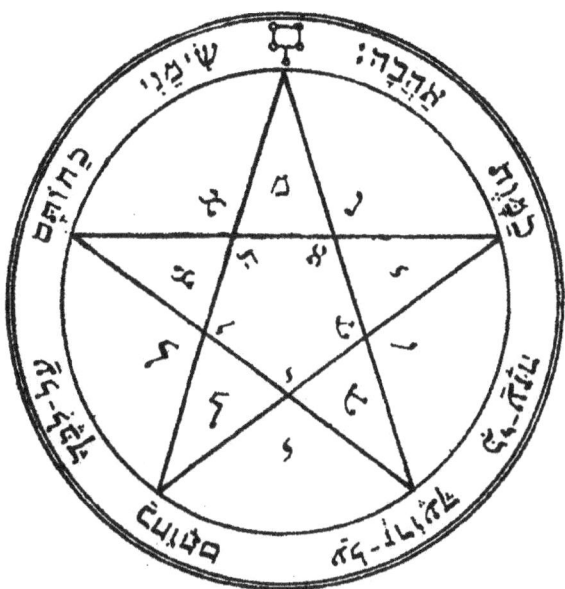

This, the second pentacle of Venus, is useful for the acquiring of those things associated with the office of Venus. Love, Friendship, Honour, Grace and Peace.

The vesicle around the talisman is from *Canticles* 8:6.

> '*Place me a signet upon thy heart, As a signet upon thine arm, For love is strong as death.*'

## THE THIRD PENTACLE OF VENUS

The third pentacle of Venus will promote love and friendship to the wearer thereof. Its angel is Monaciel who must be invoked on the day and during the hour of Venus.

The names IHVH and ADONAI are in the middle and either side of the triangles. Also present are the names Ruach and Achides, and also the angelic names Aegalmiel, Monachiel and Degaliel.

The vesicle is from the first book of the bible - *Genesis* 1:28

> 'And the Elohim blessed them, And the Elohim said unto them Be ye fruitful and multiply
> And replenish the earth and subdue it.'

The angelic sigils are given below

Aegalmiel          Monachiel          Degaliel

## THE FOURTH PENTACLE OF VENUS

The fourth pentacle of Venus will compel the spirits of Venus to be obedient to one's will. With this they will bring to you any person so desired.

At the four angles of the figure are the letters forming the name YHVH. Also the names of the spirits of Venus Schii – Eli – Ayib whose seals are given below.

The vesicle is from *Genesis* 2:23

> 'This is bone of my bones and flesh of my flesh.
> And they two were one flesh.'

Schii                               Eli                              Ayib

## THE FIFTH PENTACLE OF VENUS

The fifth pentacle of Venus will promote love if shown unto any person, when correctly made.

Around the central square written in the magical script 'Passing of the *River*,' are the names Elohim El Gbil.

The surrounding vesicle is from *Psalm* 22:14

> 'My heart is like wax
> It is melted in the midst of my bowels.'

## THE FIRST PENTACLE OF MERCURY

The God Name for all Mercurial talismans: Elohim Tzabaoth meaning *God of Hosts*

Archangel: Raphael meaning *Healer of God*

Order of Angels: Beni Elohim

Colour: Orange

Incense: Lavender

This, the first pentacle of Mercury, will invoke the spirits of Mercury and will perform those things appertaining to the office of the planet Mercury.

The names of the Mercury spirits Yekahel and Agiel are associated with this talismanic figure and are found herein.

Yekahel                                   Agiel

## THE SECOND PENTACLE OF MERCURY

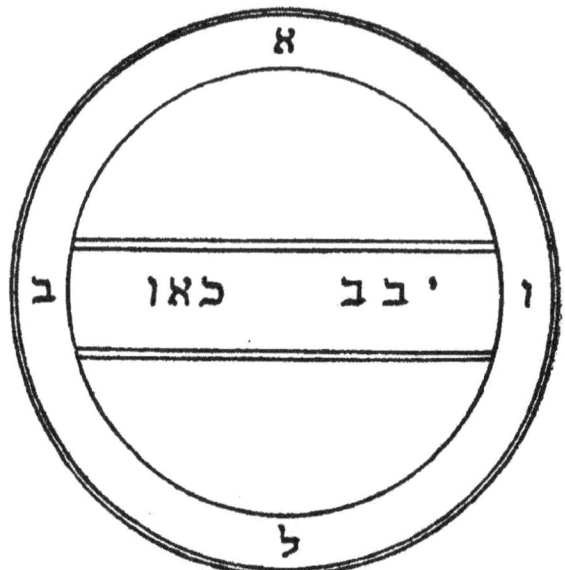

The second pentacle of Mercury will grant anything that is not of the office of the previous pentacles. The spirits give answers readily but are not easy to see.

Its angel is Boel whose seal is below.

Boel

## THE THIRD PENTACLE OF MERCURY

This pentacle will invoke the aid of those Mercurial spirits here written around. Kokaviel from the Hebrew word for Mercury - Kokab, Ghedoriah, Savaniah and Chokmahiel from Chokmah – wisdom.

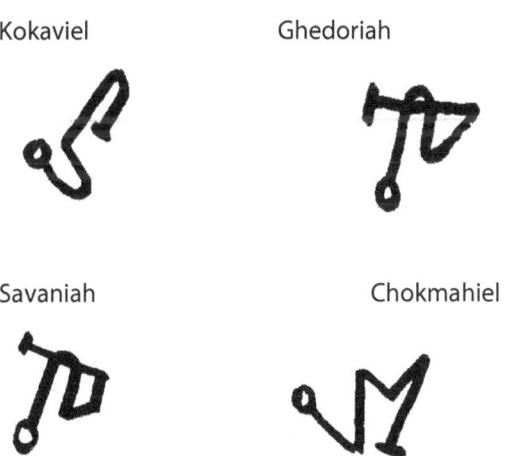

## THE FOURTH PENTACLE OF MERCURY

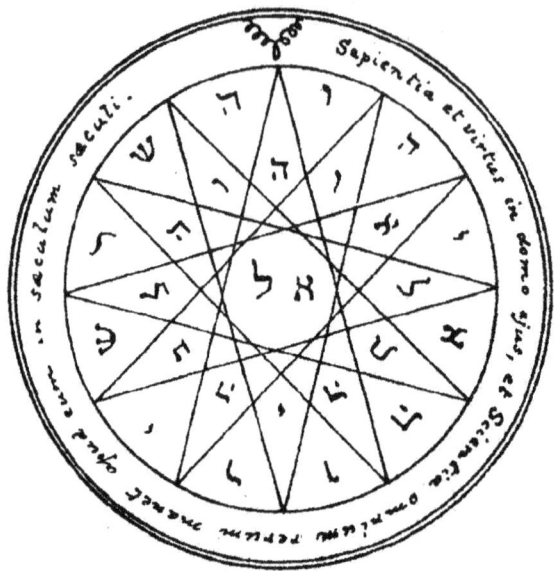

The fourth pentacle of Mercury is useful to gain the understanding and knowledge of all things created and to seek out and penetrate into hidden things. Also it will help in the control of mercurial spirits who will attend to one's will in all matters relating to the office of Mercury.

The name of God EL is placed in the middle of the talisman. Around the nine-pointed star is the sentence *'YHVH fix thou the volatile and let there be unto the void restriction.'*

The vesicle around the talisman says

> *'Wisdom and virtue are in his house And the knowledge of all things Remained with him forever.'*

## THE FIFTH PENTACLE OF MERCURY

This the last pentacle of Mercury will command the spirits of Mercury and will also open all doors and remove obstruction from areas of one's life. For nothing that it encounters may resist its power when properly made.

In the pentacle are the names EL – AB and IHVH signifying Lord God and Father.

The verse is from *Psalm* 24:7

> *'Lift up your heads O ye gates and be ye lift up ye everlasting doors for the King of Glory shall come in.'*

## THE FIRST PENTACLE OF THE MOON

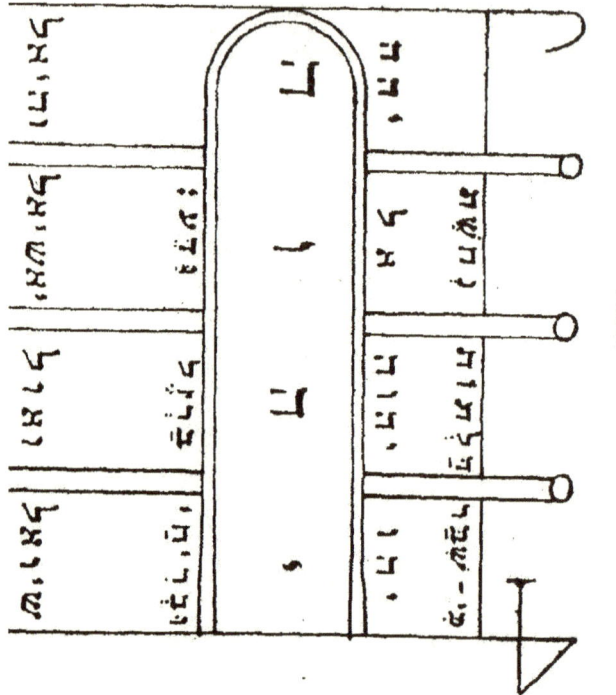

The God Name for all lunar talismans: Shaddai El Chai meaning *Almighty Living God*

Archangel: Gabriel meaning *Strong One of God*

Order of Angels: Kerubim

Colour: Purple or Silver

Incense: Jasmine

The first pentacle of the Moon will bring forth those spirits who are of the Moon. It will also remove obstacles and open all doors to success. The talisman is drawn as a gate and in the centre is written IHVH. Also within the talisman are the names IHV – IHVH and IHH. On the left of the talisman are the names of the angels, Schioel, Vaol, Yashiel and Yehiel, whose seals are given below.

The vesicle given is from *Psalm* 107:16

> 'He hath broken the gates of brass And smitten the bars of iron in sunder.'

Schioel

Vaol

Yashiel

Yehiel

## THE SECOND LUNAR PENTACLE

The second pentacle of the moon will preserve against all danger by water. It will also control all lunar spirits.

Written in the figure is the name of God EL and also the angel Abariel whose seal is given below.

The verse is from *Psalm* 56:11

> 'In Elohim have I put my trust,
> I will not fear what man can do unto me.'

Abariel

## THE THIRD PENTACLE OF THE MOON

The third pentacle of the moon if made aright will serve to protect the wearer from all danger and perils when travelling.

In the centre of the figure are the names Aub and Vevaphel.

The verse is from *Psalm* 40:13

   'Be pleased O YHVH to deliver me, O YHVH make haste to help me.'

Vevaphel

## THE FOURTH PENTACLE OF THE MOON

This, the fourth pentacle of the Moon, will defend from all evil and will protect from evil both body and soul. Its angel is Sophiel who will teach of the virtue of herbs and stones.

Within the talisman is the Divine Name EHIEH ASHER EHIEH and also the angelic names Yahel and Sophiel.

The verse is *Jeremiah* 17:18

> *'Let them be confounded who persecute me and let me not be confounded let them fear and not I.'*

## THE FIFTH PENTACLE OF THE MOON

The fifth pentacle of the Moon will grant dreams which will answer questions. Its angel is Iachadiel who will also cause destruction and loss at the command of the conjuror. He will also summon the souls of the dead and bring them to your presence.

The names within the talisman are IHVH and ELOHIM. Also the names of the angels Iachadiel and Azarel.

The verse is from *Psalm* 68:1

> 'Let God arise and let his enemies be scattered let them also who hate him flee before him'

Iachadiel                    Azarel

## THE SIXTH PENTACLE OF THE MOON

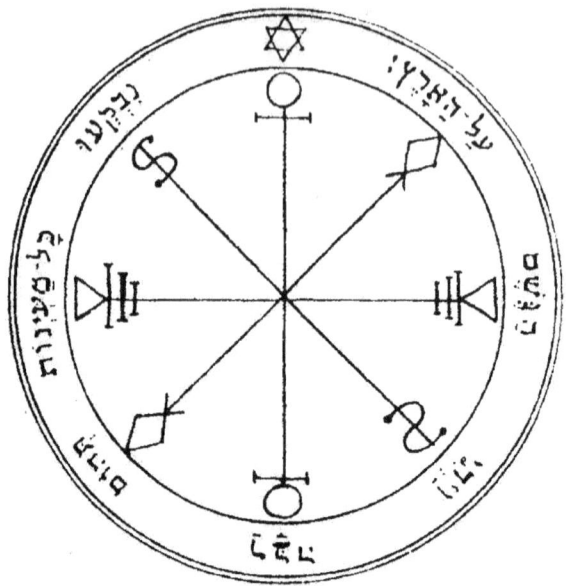

This, the last pentacle of the Moon, is good to promote wet weather and rain. It must be placed in water and it will rain as long as it is therein. For this it will be better if it is engraved on the day and during the hour of the Moon on a silver plate.

Around the periphery of the talisman is a verse from the *Book of Genesis* 7:11–12

> 'And all the fountains of the Great Deep were broken up and the rain was upon the earth.'

CHAPTER THREE

# Modus Operandi

*'Therefore by the name of the Living God, who hath formed the heavens above and the earth below,
We command ye come unto us from all places..'*

Having chosen the talisman to work with and having constructed it during the day and the hour of the planet that governs it, we must now, having created it on the outer levels, empower it from the inner realms from which all magic flows. This is where our magic becomes a divine arte rather than a mere science. Ritual with its attendant imagery and drama becomes the language of the subtle levels of consciousness that are beyond the everyday. And it is these levels that we need to work with and to move for our magic to manifest as we will, regardless of its hue or its creed. Thus we need good concentration and visualisation skills; we need a firm commitment to our magic and an undaunted belief in its ultimate successful outcome.

We must know that our magic is true and that there cannot be any other outcome other than our will. It is working at these levels, which can become exhausting and even disturbing, that will make our magic come to birth. It is not easy but the skills can be learnt and developed if one has the patience. As the late Israel Regardie remarked *'it is determination and patience which are the keys.'*

If you are a member of a coven or occult group that are worthy of their salt, or simply a lone student with some experience, you will no doubt appreciate these points, but for the newcomer to our arte, take note there is no such thing as a free spell - it has to be worked for. In *Liber Noctis*, I made the remark that you need to remember that you are not God, you are, as far as fate is concerned, *'Bending the bendable,'* a point worth noting.

For some, magic can be rather a simple affair, a few tools and words and the spell is released. Whilst with other systems, such as outlined here, a more complex approach is required. Both methods are valid for it is the end result that is important. If your sense of the arte demands a more complex approach so be it, if you cannot be bothered, or find it too much, and make excuses such as, *'It's too patriarchal or difficult, it's not wicca,'* then leave it alone. These are all points that I have heard others make. Remember, our arte is not for everyone but only for those who are prepared to go and get it, and then work with it. As it was once said to me when I was young, *'The world belongs to those who are prepared to get off their arse and go and get it.'*

Equally I will say that it is the same with magic. When magical energies are set loose do they work straight away or do they take time to work? I have heard asked *'Do things go wrong or will I end up being damaged in some way?'* Again common enough themes; firstly magic is not for the faint-hearted nor is it for the easily daunted. Which will by its very nature make it exclusive and thus not for the majority of people unless they change their attitudes or basic nature which is unlikely for many, but not impossible. Magic is like lightning, it takes the shortest route to earth. Therefore be very clear what it is that you are working for because it may not be what you want when you get it, and you cannot send it back. You will need to have a firm grip on life and everyday events. If you cannot cope with life and see magic as some kind of bolt hole, where you can prop up your own identity to yourself and others in a world of make believe, then you are the type of person who is more readily going to be led astray or come to harm. Primarily through delusions, self deceit and also sometimes, through adverse psychic phenomena and haunting. But as an occultist these should be within your scope to clean up and put right. Thus harmony is restored.

Assuming that you have the four elemental weapons and a space to work. Let the altar cloth and candles be of the appropriate colour, if not let them be white. Also a consecrated sword and wand if evocation to the shewstone is your method of working. Let the working space be clean and uncluttered. On the floor make out a circle ideally nine foot diameter if not use what space you have that is available. Draw a smaller circle inside the first, six inches apart from the first circle, so you now have a double circle with the smaller one being inside. Within the lines of the first circle write the names of God and the Archangelic names that govern the working.

Then having bathed and purified mind, body and soul consecrate the salt and water first and also the incense and fire in the form of burning charcoal. Dedicate the candles and if working with the evocation of the planetary spirits into the shewstone the talismanic figure with the seals of the spirits on the back of it will have to be consecrated and placed under the shewstone. Preferably with a cord of white silk, mark out a triangle on the top of the altar in which will sit the shewstone. If you are working with the Middle Pillar, a less complex method of consecration will be given shortly. In this case ignore the shewstone advice as this is not applicable. Perform the Lesser Banishing Ritual of the Pentagram, also known as LBRP. The salt and water are now sprinkled around the circle's edge with suitable wording and fire with burning incense is treated accordingly. The silken triangle must be conjured and made effective for the task of confining those spirits until *'Licensed to depart.'* The compass points are consecrated, as is the circle that is raised. A statement of the aim of the working is given and following this an invocation of God for the success of the work. Prayers and invocations deemed appropriate to the working are performed. Having consecrated the talisman with fire and water, trace a planetary Hexagram over it with the wand as you invoke the planet's energies to conjure the spirits of the talisman to perform your will.

Perform the Middle Pillar meditation and see therein your magic manifesting according to your will. Raising the wand, a symbol of your will, pour the coloured light which will be of the colour of the planet concerned into the talismanic figure. See it lock on to it as a shining ball. Let your gaze see in this ball of light that which you are working for come to pass. Let your conviction be firm and sure, so that the future has no escape as your will comes to birth. See the talisman absorb the light and be charged. Take the talisman to the four compass points and call upon the elements to note that it is a talisman of whatever planet it is and that it is duly consecrated too.

If working with an evocation the spirits are conjured into the shewstone wherefrom they are instructed in their duties and their energies are bound to the talisman. Afterwards do not forget under any circumstances to give the License to Depart so that they can go back to their proper realms and habitations. All energies are dismissed, whichever method of working and prayers of thanks are given before closing the circle down and a banishing with the LBRP.

The talismanic figure is kept somewhere safe, some people will place it in a cloth bag of the planet's colour or in their wallet. Wherever you decide to keep it, it does not want to be disturbed; rather like planting a seed in the ground leave it alone and it will grow but at the same time keep an eye on it. When it has performed its duties and it is to be destroyed, thank the energies involved and let them go. The talisman can be buried with the intent that as it rots so it is deactivated.

CHAPTER FOUR

# Non nobis Domini

> 'May Holy Mikael, the Archangel of God and Midael and Mirael the Chiefs and Captains of the Celestial Army be my aid in the operation I am about to perform.'

## LESSER BANISHING RITUAL OF THE PENTAGRAM

Face East: Kabbalistic Cross

Raise your right hand above the crown of your head and visualise a brilliant sphere shining. As you bring your hand down to touch your fore-head let a shaft of light travel downwards and intone ATEH (meaning thou art).

Let the light travel downwards through your body to your feet. Now touch your chest and intone MALKUTH (the kingdom).

Touch the right shoulder and intone VE-GEBURAH (and the power).

Touch the left shoulder and intone VE-GEDULAH (and the glory).

Cross hands on chest and intone LE–OLAHM AMEN (to the ages forever)

Now trace in the air a banishing pentagram, three feet high and in white light.

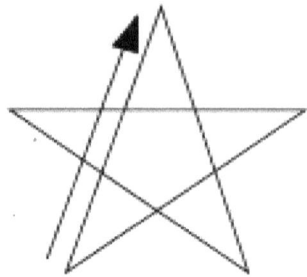

Stab the centre as you intone YHVH (yod-heh-vav-heh) and see the pentagram move out to the circumference of your working space and feel it cleaning the area that it moves across. Trace a line of light from this pentagram around to the southern quarter and here trace another one. This time as you stab the centre of it intone ADNI (ah-don-i). Bringing the line around to the west trace another pentagram and intone EHIEH (eh-heh-yeh). The line is now taken to the north and again another pentagram is traced as the others and the word intoned is AGLA (ah-glah). Turn to face east again, tracing the last part of the circle back to your starting point and the eastern pentagram.

You now have a complete circle around the working place with charged pentagrams at the quarters. Standing in the centre stretch your arms out to form a cross. Visualise in the east a mighty yellow robed figure and say, *'Before Me Raphael.'* Sense the element blowing from this quarter.

Behind in the west is a mighty blue robed figure holding a chalice. Hear water playing from this quarter and say, *'Behind Me Gabriel.'*

At your right see a mighty red robed figure bearing a drawn sword and feel warmth emanating from this quarter and say, *'On My Right Mikael.'*

To your left see a figure that is dressed in the dark colours of the earth. The figure is holding a sheaf of corn and other things of the earth. Say, *'On My left Auriel.'* See these figures standing outside the circle at its edge and looking in.

Visualise behind you a six pointed star thus:

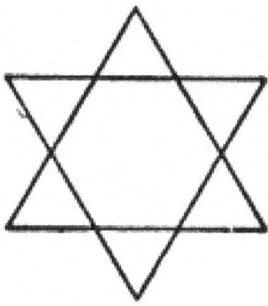

Declare:

'About me flame the pentagrams, behind me shines the six-rayed star.'

Perform the Kabbalistic Cross as at the beginning of the working.

## MIDDLE PILLAR

The Middle Pillar is one of the most important magical exercises in the Western Magical Traditions, as it is the key to many other magical workings. While it may seem complex it does become easier with regular use. If combined with the LBRP it becomes a good daily exercise which will help to strengthen the aura and to promote a positive state of mind. The Middle Pillar is based on the Kabbalistic Tree of Life and it will be worth your while studying the writings of Israel Regardie, particularly his work *Middle Pillar*, and also *Foundations of Practical Magic*. The Middle Pillar can be used for the consecration and the charging of talismans and it will be found to be useful in acts of evocation.

Visualise above your head a shinning sphere of brilliant white light. Try to place your consciousness therein if only momentarily. Intone silently or otherwise the wording 'EHIEH' (eh-he-eh), meaning *'I am.'*

Now bring a column of light from this sphere downwards through the head and let it blossom at the throat in a lavender colour sphere. Intone 'YHVH ELOHIM' (yod-heh-vav-heh-elohim), meaning *'Lord God.'*

Bring the light down to your chest again and visualise the ball of light in the colours of the sun and intone 'YHVH ALOAH VE DAATH' (yod-heh-vav-heh el-oa ve da-art), meaning *'God made manifest in the sphere of the mind.'*

Let the light continue downwards to your genital region and here it forms a purple coloured ball and intone 'SHADDAI EL CHAI' (sha-dye el kye) meaning *'Almighty Living God.'*

Finally the light flows to your feet and forms a ball of earth coloured light. Here you intone 'ADONAI HA ARETZ' (ah-doh-nye ha ah-retz), meaning *'Lord of this Earth.'* As you intone each name try and feel it vibrating in the imaginary sphere also place your consciousness there even if just momentarily.

Go back to Kether and concentrate thereon, and as you breathe out let the light flow down your left side to your feet, pause and as you breathe in let it flow up your right side back to Kether; let this be done thrice. Following the same sequence as you breathe out let the light flow down across the front of your body to your feet, pause and whilst breathing in let the light flow up the back of your body to Kether, thus completing the circuit.

After bringing the Middle Pillar into play, the aura can be flooded with the planetary colour that you are working with whilst you intone the God Names and the names of the archangel associated with the planet. See what it is that you want to happen, and know it to be true as you pour the energies into the talisman before you.

## THE EN-HALLOWING OF THE COMPASS POINTS

All workings of a magical nature that are here described will need to be performed within a circle that has been set apart from the everyday and made holy. This is the function of the following working and can be adapted for a wide range of magical works.

> Lesser Banishing Ritual of the Pentagram (LBRP)
>
> Consecration of the salt and water
>
> Trace over the salt a banishing pentagram whilst intoning:
>> 'Let all malignancy and hindrance be cast forth hence from so that only good may enter herein.'
>
> Trace invoking pentagram saying:
>> 'Wherefore I do bless thee that thou mayest aid me with this my holy act of magic.
>> In the names of the God most High.'
>
> Using the same pentagram over the water say:
>> 'I exorcise thee O creature of water that thou cast out from thee all spirits of the world of phantasm. So that only good may enter herein.
>> Wherefore I do bless thee and I do consecrate thee in the names of the God Most High.'
>
> Pour the salt into the water:
>
> Sprinkle around the edge of the circle saying:
>> 'First the Priest(ess) who governeth the works of fire must sprinkle with the waters of the loud resounding sea.'
>
> Cense with incense
>> 'And when after all the phantasms have vanished thou shalt see the holy and formless fire,
>> the fire that flashes through the hidden depths of the universe.
>> Hear thou the voice of fire.'
>
> Return to the centre of the circle and face east.

Perform the Kabbalistic Cross and trace in the air the active invoking pentagram of spirit before making the invoking pentagram of

Air. See the Spirit pentagram in white and the air pentagram in yellow.

Intoning EXARP (EX-AR-PEH) whilst tracing spirit pentagram and touch the centre thereof saying AHIH (Eh-HE-YEH)

With the air pentagram whilst tracing it intone ORO IBAH AO-ZODPI (ORO-EE-BAH-HA-AY-O-ZOD-PEH)

Stab the centre of the second pentagram saying 'YHVH.'

Bring a line from the pentagram around to the south and trace another set of pentagrams. Active spirit in white, the fire pentagram in red.

Intone for spirit BITOM (BAY-EE-TO-EM) Centre AHIH

With the fire pentagram whilst tracing it intone OIP TEAA PEDOCE (O-EE-PEH-TEE-AH-AH-PED-O-KEY) Centre ELOHIM (EL-O-HEEM).

Bring the line around to the west trace a third set of pentagrams. Spirit passive in white then water in blue.

Intone HCOMA with spirit pentagram: AGLA at centre: Saying with the water pentagram: EMPEH ARSEL GAIOL (EM-PEH-AY-AR-SEL-GAY-EE-OL), Centre EL.

Bring the line around to the north and trace both pentagrams here at this quarter, invoking spirit passive pentagram and then the earth invoking pentagram.

Wording for the spirit pentagram is NANTA (EN-AH-EN-TAA) Centre AGLA:

Whilst tracing the earth pentagram EMOR DIAL HECTAGA (EM-ORR-DI-AL-HEC-TAY-GAH) Centre ADNI:

Bring the line around to the east where you started from to complete the circle.

Repeat the Archangelic invocations as in the Lesser Banishing Ritual of the Pentagram and also the Kabbalistic Cross. Facing east declare:

> *'HOLY ART THOU LORD OF CREATION FOR THY GLORY FLOWS OUT*
> *TO THE ENDS OF THE CREATION REJOICING BE WITH ME NOW AS I PERFORM THIS WORK WHICH I DEDICATE UNTO THEE.'*

Then follows an invocation in Enochian, create something of your own here if so desired but stay with the spirit of the invocation.

> OL SONUF VAORSAGI GOHO IADA BALTA ELEXARPEH CO-MANANU TABITOM ZODAKARA EKA ZODAKARA OD ZODA MERANU ODO KIKLE QAA PIAPE PIAMOEL OD VAOAN.

Pronounced as:

> 'OH-EL-SO-NOOF-VAY-OH-AIR-SAH-JEE-GOH-HOH-EE-AH- DAH-BAL-TAH-EL-EX-AR-PEH-HEH-CO-MAH-NAH-NOO-TAH- BEE-TOH-EM-ZOHD-AH-KAH-RAH-EH-KAH-ZOD-AH-KAH-RAY- OH-DAH-ZOHD-AH-MER-AH-AH-NOO-OH-DOH-KEE-KLAY-KAH- AH-PEE-AH-PAY-PE-AH-MOH-ELL-OH-DAH-VAY-OH-AH-NOO.'

Meaning:

> 'I reign over you saith the God of Justice, ELEXARPEH-COMANANU-TABITOM
> Move therefore and show thyselves.
> Appear unto us; open the mysteries of thy creation the balance of righteousness and truth.'

Still facing the east intone the following or something else of your own creation.

> 'I invoke thee, ye angels of the Celestial Spheres, whose dwelling is in the invisible. For thou art the guardians of the Universe be thou guardians of this my sacred space.
> Keep far from me the evil and the unbalanced,
> Strengthen and inspire me so that I may preserve unsullied this abode of the mysteries of God.
> Let my sphere be pure and holy that I may enter therein and become a partaker of the secrets of the light divine.'

Contemplate the sanctity and sacredness of your space for a few moments, and then proceed with your working. Afterwards close with the following after thanking the energies that you have been working with for their assistance.

Work follows. To close give thanks for the energies that you have worked with and dismiss to their proper abodes and habitations causing no harm nor any fear.

> 'NON NOBIS DOMINI NON NOBIS SED NOMINI TUA DA HONORUM PROPTER BENIGNATATUM PROPTER FIDE TUAM.'

Meaning:

> 'Not unto us O Lord, not unto us but unto Thy Name be the Glory for Your Mercy and Faith.'

## THE ARTE OF EVOCATION

This is without doubt the most complex but spectacular act of the arte and one that is really the domain of those who have some experience and understanding of the magical arte. Whilst some grimoires will suggest that you conjure into a triangle others leave the spirit to simply manifest whilst the conjuror is safe within their circle. With this work we will do neither. By creating our triangle of arte on our altar, with the shewstone therein and the consecrated seal of the planet there under, we can work with this for the consecration of the talisman.

The altar is laid out as such:

**East**

| Candle | Oil of Abra-Melin | Candle |
|---|---|---|

Wand

| Pentacle with salt | | Knife with black hilt |
|---|---|---|

Equal sided triangle[1]

| Book of Arte | Chalice | Censer |
|---|---|---|

Sword

---

[1] This is marked out with white cord and has the shewstone placed therein with talisman or sigil underneath

Having cleaned your working space and marked out your circle, you must now bathe and purify the body. Afterwards pour over yourself a jug of consecrated water whilst intoning the following from *Psalm 51*.

> 'ASPERGES ME DOMINI HYSSOPO. LAVABIS ME ET SUPER NEALVUM ET DEALABOUR.'

Meaning:

> 'Purge me with hyssop O Lord and I shall be clean, wash me and I will be whiter than snow.'

Don a clean white robe saying:

> 'By the figurative mysteries of these garments I will clothe me with the armour of salvation in the strength of the God Most High.
> ANCOR: AMACOR: AMIDES: THEODONIAS: ANITOR: that my desired end may be effected through Thy strength O Adonai unto Whom be the praise and the glory forever. Amen.'

With Abra-Melin oil you now mark your brow and give a prayer for the success of the working.

Continue with the Kabbalistic Cross and the LBRP, consecration of salt and water, dedication of candles, incense and fire (burning charcoal). The triangle must be consecrated also with the consecrated talismanic figure under the shewstone. Do not cross over the boundary of the triangle until all energies have been returned to their proper place of being. To consecrate the triangle firstly bless and dedicate with the holy water and salt, then with fire in the form of the censer going around the triangle. This is done with the firm conviction that nothing will cross it. Then trace around the triangle with the sword or knife with the black handle and visualise strongly that a barrier is forming over which nothing will cross and that those energies that make manifest therein will be obedient unto your will and that they will return to their realms when they are Licensed to Depart, causing no harm nor fear. As you conjure the triangle let it be in the names of TETRAGRAMMATON: PRIMEUMATEON: ANAPHAXETON: and by the Holy Name of the Archangel Mikael.

Carry on creating the magical circle and declare the purpose of the working. Perform the Middle Pillar with the clear intent that you are invoking your highest aspect of your being that will aid you in this working and that you are placing the work under the auspices of the God Most High. If you are familiar with this working and can visualise the *'Lightning Flash'* descending and establishing the other Sephiroth of the Tree of Life then do so. Place even if momentarily your consciousness within the sphere of Kether above your head and intone the following triumphal invocation and identification:

> 'I AM HE THE BORNLESS SPIRIT HAVING SIGHT IN THE FEET STRONG AND THE IMMORTAL FIRE!
> I AM HE THE TRUTH
> I AM HE WHO HATES THAT EVIL SHOULD BE WROUGHT IN THE WORLD
> I AM HE WHO LIGHTENETH AND THUNDERETH
> I AM HE FROM WHOM IS THE SHOWER OF THE LIFE ON EARTH
> I AM HE THE BEGETTER AND THE MANIFESTER UNTO THE LIGHT
> THE HEART GIRT WITH A SERPENT IS MY NAME!'

See your aura glow as you intone the following:

> 'COME THOU FORTH AND FOLLOW ME AND MAKE ALL SPIRITS SUBJECT UNTO ME
> SO THAT EVERY SPIRIT OF THE FIRMAMENT AND OF THE ETHER UPON THE EARTH AND ON DRY LAND
> OR IN THE WATER OR RUSHING AIR OR OF RUSHING FIRE AND EVERY SPELL OF GOD THE VAST AND MIGHTY ONE
> MAY BE MADE OBEDIENT UNTO ME! IAO SABAO! SUCH ARE THE WORDS!'

Whilst this working is demanding it is of importance in establishing and strengthening your spiritual links with those higher aspects of your being. Thus it is not your everyday you, but you at your most potent and God-inspired self that now commands. Now flood your aura with the planetary colour whilst intoning the relevant God Name and Archangelic name of the planet that you are working with.

Trace in the air over the shewstone, but not crossing its boundary, the planetary symbol. Use your wand which is a symbol of your will in motion, and declare the following conjuration. This can be said several times if need be and as the tensions develop and the subtle links are formed between you and the spirit's realms concentrate on the shewstone and let the energies manifest. Whilst there are traditional forms for the spirits to manifest they do not always do so and will appear in other guises. Test the spirit by using the God Name and the Archangelic name to declare its name and office. If it is your spirit it will stay, if not it will go at the use of the God Name.

'I...XYZ....COMMAND, CONSTRAIN AND INVOKE THEE O SPIRIT (name) BY THE POWER OF THE HOLY NAME OF GOD (God Name) AND BY THE MIGHT OF THE HOLY ARCHANGEL (name) TO MAKE MANIFEST ACCORDING TO MY WILL APPEARING IN COMELY FORM COMING IN PEACE AND HARMONY HARMING NONE NOR GIVING FEAR TO ANY.
FURTHER MORE THAT THOU DEPARTEST
FOR THY REALMS WHEN THOU ART LICENSED TO DO SO GOING IN PEACE AND CAUSING NO HARM
THIS BEING FOR THE GLORY OF GOD AND HARMETH NONE.
SO MOTE IT BE!'

Gaze silently into the shewstone and visualise the sigil of the spirit. Silently call unto it and wait. Note that the spirit is evoked by a strict pecking order, God Name then Archangelic and Planetary Intelligence. This represents the Kabbalistic four worlds of creation. Atziluth, God Name pure spirit of the energies invoked, Briah creative Archangelic (gets things done), Yetzirah, forms Angelic (does the work) and Assiah, the world we inhabit. Each level corresponds to the letters of the name YHVH. If nothing appears to be happening do not worry, just because you cannot see the spirit does not mean that it is not there. Repeat your invocation again and put more incense on the censer. If you feel that nothing is happening or there are no signs of a manifestation move on to the next invocation which is longer and more intense.

Holding the wand upon high declare:

'IN THE GREAT NAME OF GOD (God Name) WHICH RULETH OVER THE FORCES OF (planet)
I INVOKE THEE O HOLY (Archangel) OF THE PLANET (state)
THAT BY THINE AID THE PLANETARY INTELLIGENCE (name) CAUSETH THE SPIRIT (xyz)
TO ARISE FROM THEIR ABODES AND HABITATIONS TO MAKE MANIFEST IN THIS SHEWSTONE IN THE TRIANGLE OF ARTE HERE BEFORE ME ACCORDING UNTO MY WILL.
FURTHER MORE THAT THEY COMEST IN PEACE AND DEPART UNTO THEIR PROPER REALMS AND HABITATIONS WHEN LICENSED TO DO SO.
THEREFORE LET THE SPIRIT (xyz) ARISE NOW BEFORE ME SPEAKING WORDS OF TRUTH AND UNDERSTANDING AND TO ACCOMPLISH MY WILL ACCORDINGLY.
ARISE O SPIRIT...(xyz)... ARISE!
FOR I COMMAND THEE BY THE MIGHT OF THE HOLY NAME (God

> *Name)* TO APPEAR NOW WITHIN THIS SHEWSTONE OF THE ARTE HERE BEFORE ME!
> *(xyz)* ARISE AND COME FORTH FROM THY REALMS AND THY HABITATIONS!
> MAKE MANIFEST O SPIRIT *(xyz)* ACCORDING UNTO MY WILL.
> FOR I EVOKE THEE BY THE MIGHTY NAME *(God Name)* AND BY THE MIGHT OF THE HOLY ARCHANGEL *(Name)* AND BY THE INTELLIGENCE OF THE PLANET *(name)* THEREFORE LET THE POWERS OF THE REALMS OF *(planet)* BE OBEDIENT UNTO THE MIGHTY NAME *(God Name)* THEREFORE IN AND BY THE SAME NAME AND BY THE HOLY POWERS OF THAT REALM I DO SUMMON STIR AND CALL THEE UP!!

By now you should have a good head of steam and be well tuned in to the spirit and their realms. This empathy will help the concentration of your will, the attention and atmosphere which by now will be quite palpable: all play their part in creating the right conditions to aid the spirit's manifestation. But is it all imagination? If your preparations have included fasting for twenty-four hours some will think that this will produce hallucinations more so if you are stupid enough to use drugs in your rites which I strongly do not advocate. After all we are after a magical experience not a chemical one. Leave the drugs to those who wish to delude themselves they have nothing to offer this type of magic, particularly as they, the drugs, rob the will.

As the spirit's manifestation takes place greet it with the names of God that govern its sphere and it will declare itself. Treat the entity with firm courtesy and give it its duties which must be within its office, and thank it and give it the License to Depart. Even if you feel that no spirit has appeared it is important that you still give the License to Depart, as you do not want any stray energies hanging around.

License to Depart:

> 'THEREFORE O SPIRIT *(xyz)*
> I GIVE THEE LICENSE TO DEPART TO YOUR PROPER REALMS AND HABITATIONS. GO NOW IN PEACE AND BE THOU READY
> TO ATTEND TO MY WILL WHEN I CALL THEE. IN THE NAMES *(God Name)*
> AND IN THE NAME OF THE HOLY ARCHANGEL *(name)* AND BY THE NAME OF THINE INTELLIGENCE *(name)* DEPART NOW AND GO IN PEACE CAUSING NO HARM TO ANYONE NOR ANYTHING.
> AND LET THE BLESSING OF THE GOD MOST HIGH BE UPON THEE AND LET THERE BE GRACE AND HARMONY BETWEEN US NOW

*AND FOR EVERMORE SO MOTE IT BE!'*

Watch as the energies fade away and give thanks to the planetary energies invoked in this working. Then declare the following:

'NON NOBIS DOMINI etc'

Re-consecrate with fire and water and perform the LBRP.

Declare:

*'I SET FREE ANY SPIRITS
THAT HAVE BEEN IMPRISONED BY THIS CEREMONY GO IN PEACE TO YOUR ABODES AND HABITATIONS AND LET THE BLESSINGS OF GOD MOST HIGH
BE UPON THEE AND ABOUT THEE NOW AND FOREVER MORE.
ADONAI ACHED – THE LORD IS ONE!'*

Working at this level is demanding to say the least, the levels of concentration must be high as must be your intent, both of which must be maintained throughout without wavering. Creating a flow without interruptions is important, you do not want to stop and wonder *'what next?'* If the inks that you have used to draw your seals have had some fluid condenser added to them this will help to hold any magical charge that has been aroused and is empowering your talisman. It is useful to have both inks and pen solely for the arte, having dedicated both items to the arte. For constructive workings use a waxing moon and a waning moon for negative workings. I do not make any judgment on the morality of an action, magic has no morals but the energies can be used for either good or bad action. It is the operator who must question their own motives.

After the working, record it and have something to eat and drink; as this will help to *'earth'* you and re-establish you in the everyday world. How long does magic take to work is like asking how long is a piece of string. I have known matters to be resolved within a period of twenty-four hours, and I have also known matters to take months before they come to birth. Yet despite magical success the ultimate goal is one's union with the Godhead from which all things flow and unto whom all things return; the final destiny. Developing magical skills will, (to quote Chris Bray from the Sorcerer's Apprentice, twenty-five years ago, remember them?) *'Expand Minds and Raise Consciousness'*. If you manage to lift yourself above the everyday and see a glimpse of the *'Bigger Picture'* which we are all part of, most of the daily trivia and annoyances will be seen in their true light as being of no real consequence and it will become apparent how much time and energy we all waste on irrelevance; which we could be using for good effect elsewhere in our lives. But as your magic evolves within your soul you will realise that the………………..

> *'Man of Religion will Believe in God*
> *But the Magician Knows God!'*

## Pentagrams

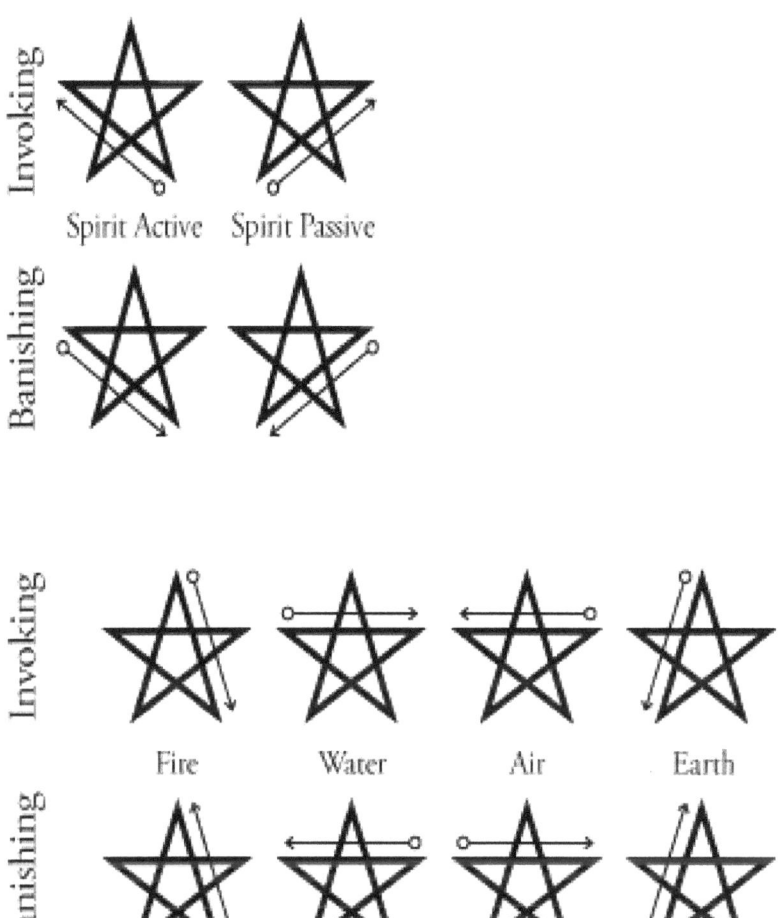

# Hexagrams

| Hexagram | Banish | Invoke |
|---|---|---|
| Saturn | | |
| Jupiter | | |
| Mars | | |
| Sun | | |

| | | |
|---|---|---|
| Venus | | |
| Mercury | | |
| Moon | | |

# Index

## A

Abariel .................................. 62
Acheliah ........................... 49, 50
Adoniel ................................. 29
Aegalmiel ............................. 52
Agiel ..................................... 55
Air ................................... 16, 76
Anachiel ............................... 19
Anazachia ............................ 19
Angelic Writing ..................... 43
Aralim, Angels ................ 17, 24
Arauchiah ............................ 19
Arehanah ........................ 21, 22
Ariel, Ruler of Earth .... 31, 47, 48
Assiah, World ....................... 81
Atziluth, World ..................... 81
Auphanim, Angels ................ 24
Ayib ..................................... 53
Azarel ................................... 65

## B

Bariel .................................... 29
Barrett, Francis ..................... 13
Bartzabel, Planetary Spirit ..... 33
Bartzachiah ..................... 33, 34
Beni Elohim, Angels .......... 24, 55
Boel ..................................... 56
Briah, World ......................... 81

## C

Cancer .................................. 29
*Canticles* 8.6 ......................... 51
cedar .................................... 25
Celestial Script ...................... 40
Chaioth Ha–Qadesch, Angels . 24
Chasan .................................. 47
Chashmalim, Angels ......... 24, 25
Cherub, Ruler of Air .............. 31
Cherub, Ruler of Earth .......... 48
Chokmah .............................. 57
Chokmahiel .......................... 57
*Clavicula Salomonis* .. 12, *See Key of Solomon*

## D

*Daniel* 4.34 ........................... 43
Davachiah ....................... 25, 26
Degaliel ................................ 52
*Deuteronomy* 10.17 .............. 21
*Deuteronomy* 109.18 ............ 20
*Deuteronomy* 4.6 .................. 20
dragon's blood ...................... 33

## E

Earth ............................... 16, 74
Eleazar ................................. 12
Eli 53
Elohim, Angels ................ 24, 49
Eschiel ............................ 33, 34

# Index

*Ezekiel* 1.1 ................................ 30

**F**

Fire ........................................... 16
frankincense ........................... 41

**G**

Gabriel, Archangel ............ 60, 72
*Genesis* 1.28 ........................... 52
*Genesis* 2.23 ........................... 53
*Genesis* 7.11–12 ..................... 66
Ghedoriah .............................. 57
Golden Dawn .......................... 13

**H**

Haniel, Archangel .................. 49
Hexagram ........................ 27, 69

**I**

Iachadiel ................................. 65
incense ................. 68, 75, 79, 81
Ithuriel ............................. 33, 34

**J**

jasmine ................................... 60
*Jeremiah* 17.18 ...................... 64
*John* 1.4 ................................. 35
Jupiter 14, 25, 27, 28, 29, 31, 32, 86

**K**

Kabbalah ................................ 12
Kabbalistic Cross . 71, 73, 75, 76, 79
Kerubim .................................. 24
Kerubim, Angels ..................... 60
Kether ...................... 41, 74, 80
*Key of Solomon* ................ 11, 12
Khamael, Archangel ............... 33
Kokaviel .................................. 57

**L**

lavender .................................. 55
LBRP ......... 69, 73, 75, 79, 83, *See* Lesser Banishing Ritual of the Pentagram
*Le Livre de Salomon* ................ 12
Lesser Banishing Ritual of the Pentagram .................... 69, 76
License to Depart ............. 69, 82

**M**

Madimiel ......................... 33, 34
Malakim, Angels ............... 24, 41
Malkhiel ................................. 42
*Mars* .. 14, 33, 35, 36, 37, 38, 39, 40, 86
Mathers, Samuel Liddell MacGregor . 11, 12, 13, 30, 46
*Mercury* ... 14, 55, 56, 57, 58, 59, 87
Metatron, Archangel .............. 41
Midael .................................... 71
Middle Pillar ... 13, 69, 73, 74, 79
Mikael, Archangel . 41, 71, 72, 79
Mirael .................................... 71
Monachiel .............................. 52
*Moon* ........ 14, 60, 64, 65, 66, 87
myrhh .................................... 17

**N**

Nangariel .......................... 49, 50
Netonial ........................... 25, 26
Noaphiel ........................... 21, 22
Nogahiel ........................... 49, 50

**O**

Omeliel .................................. 19

**P**

Paimoniah .............................. 42
Parasiel ............................ 25, 26

Passing of the River ... 44, 45, 46, 54
Peterson, Joseph ..................... 11
Phorlakh ................................. 47
*Psalm* 105.32-33 ..................... 40
*Psalm* 107.16 ........................... 60
*Psalm* 110.5 ............................. 37
*Psalm* 112.3 ....................... 27, 29
*Psalm* 113.7 ............................. 32
*Psalm* 116.16–17 ..................... 48
*Psalm* 125.1 ............................. 28
*Psalm* 13.3-4 ........................... 44
*Psalm* 135.16 ........................... 46
*Psalm* 18.7 ............................... 24
*Psalm* 22.14 ............................. 54
*Psalm* 22.16-17 ........................ 31
*Psalm* 24.7 ............................... 59
*Psalm* 37.15 ............................. 39
*Psalm* 40.13 ............................. 63
*Psalm* 51 .................................. 79
*Psalm* 56.11 ............................. 62
*Psalm* 68.1 ............................... 65
*Psalm* 69.23 ............................. 46
Psalm 72.8 ............................... 18
*Psalm* 72.9 ............................... 17
*Psalm* 77.13 ............................. 36
*Psalm* 91.11-12 ........................ 45
*Psalm* 91.13 ............................. 38

### R

Rakhaniel ............................ 21, 22
Rankine, David ................. 11, 12
Raphael, Archangel .......... 55, 72
Regardie, Israel ................. 67, 73
Rekhodiah .............................. 42
Roelhaiphar ....................... 21, 22

### S

salt ............ 13, 67, 68, 75, 78, 79
Sator square ........................... 18
*Saturn* 14, 18, 19, 20, 21, 23, 24, 25, 28, 86
Savaniah ................................. 57
Schii ........................................ 53
Schioel ............................... 60, 61
Seraph, Ruler of Fire ......... 31, 48
Seraphim, Angels ............. 24, 33
Shemeshiel ............................. 42
shewstone 13, 68, 69, 78, 79, 80, 81
*Sigilum Salomonis* ................... 12
Skinner, Stephen .............. 11, 12
Socohiah ........................... 49, 50
Sophiel .................................... 64
*Sun* 14, 41, 42, 43, 44, 45, 46, 47, 86
*sword* .................... 39, 68, 72, 79

### T

Taliahad .................................. 47
Tharsis, Ruler of Water ..... 31, 48
*The Magus* .............................. 13
Tiphereth ................................ 43
triangle ........... 20, 46, 69, 78, 79
Tzadkiel, Archangel ............... 25
Tzaphkiel, Archangel ............. 17
Tzedeqiah ......................... 25, 26

### V

Vaol ................................... 60, 61
*Venus* ........ 14, 49, 52, 53, 54, 87
Vevaphel ................................. 63

### W

wand .............. 68, 69, 78, 80, 81
Water ...................................... 16

### Y

Yahel ....................................... 64
Yashiel ............................... 60, 61
Yeats, W.B. .............................. 11
Yehiel ................................ 60, 61

# Index

Yekahel .................................. 55
Yesod ..................................... 43
Yetzirah, World ...................... 81

Yophiel, Planetary Intelligence
 ............................................ 28

# FOUNDATIONS OF PRACTICAL SORCERY

**A seven-volume set of magical treatises, unabridged, comprising:**

**Vol. I - Liber Noctis**

*A Handbook of the Sorcerous Arte*

Liber Noctis explores the attitudes, training and preparation required for success in ritual, and, as the title suggests, does not shy away from the 'darker' aspects of magic. Practical, experiential, lucid and non-judgmental, this book lays the groundwork for the successful study and practice of sorcery in the modern world.

**Vol. II - Ars Salomonis**

*Being of that Hidden Arte of Solomon the King*

Ars Salomonis is a practical manual for working with the talismanic figures found in the Key of Solomon, the most significant of all grimoires. Including two methods for empowering and activating the planetary pentacles, the author makes this vital work safely accessible to beginners. It is an ideal entranceway into the grimoire tradition.

**Vol. III - Ars Geomantica**

*Being an account and rendition of the Arte of Geomantic Divination and Magic*

Ars Geomantica explores the medieval system of Geomancy, one of the simplest and most practical of the divinatory arts. The inclusion of detailed instructions on the creation of geomantic staves, elemental fluid condensers, and talismanic construction and consecration make this work a superb introduction to an extensive assortment of magical and divinatory principles.

**Vol. IV - Ars Theurgia Goetia**

*Being an account and rendition of the Arte and Praxis of the Conjuration of some of the Spirits of Solomon*

Ars Theurgia Goetia presents a precise and practical guide to working with the spirits of this neglected text from the Solomonic grimoire cycle, the Theurgia-Goetia, giving the full seals of the spirits for the first time. The complete ritual sequence of preparation, conjuration, and license to depart is lucidly demonstrated, making this work suitable for both the beginner and the experienced practitioner.

### Vol. V - Otz Chim

*The Tree of Life*

Otz Chim is a practical exploration of the magic of the Kabbalistic Tree of Life, the glyph that concentrates the essence of magic and mysticism within the Western Mystery Tradition. This book focuses on lesser-known aspects such as the angels associated with the paths, their seals, and invocations and includes the previously unavailable Massa Aborum Vitae.

### Vol. VI - Ars Speculum

*Being an Instruction on the Arte of using Mirrors and Shewstones in Magic*

Ars Speculum is a concise and practical work on the use of mirrors and shewstones in magic. In it the author explores skrying and working with the four elements of air, fire, water and earth - both with elemental condensers and different elemental creatures. Other techniques include contacting other levels of being, the conjuration of spirits, binding and ligature, and healing and protection.

### Vol. VII - Liber Terriblis

*Being an Instruction on the seventy-two Spirits of the Goetia*

Liber Terribilis is a practical study of how to work with the seventy-two spirits of the infamous seventeenth-century Grimoire, the Goetia. It also explores the vital and often neglected use of the seventy-two binding angels of the Great Name of God, the Schemhamphorasch. This volume will be of value to all levels of students and practitioners of the grimoire traditions, being based upon the work of a small group of occultists who have explored it in practice.

More information available on the Avalonia website-
**www.avaloniabooks.co.uk**

Or write to:
**BM Avalonia**
**London**
**WC1N 3XX**
**England, United Kingdom**

*Expanding the Esoteric Horizons ...*

*Avalonia* is an independent publisher producing outstanding and innovative books which push the boundaries of their subjects and illuminate the spirit of the sacred in its many manifestations.

**Explore some of the other works on the occult, mythology and magic published by Avalonia at:**

# www.avaloniabooks.co.uk

Readers who found Foundations of Practical Sorcery of interest, is likely to enjoy:

*A Collection of Magical Secrets & a Treatise of mixed Cabalah* by Stephen Skinner and David Rankine

*Climbing the Tree of Life* by David Rankine

*Living Theurgy* by Jeffrey S. Kupperman

*Practical Elemental Magick* by Sorita d'Este and David Rankine

*The Book of Gold* by David Rankine & Paul Harry Barron (trans.)

*The Book of Treasure Spirits*, edited by David Rankine

*The Complete Grimoire of Pope Honorius* by David Rankine & Paul Harry Barron (trans.)

*The Cunning Man's Handbook* by Jim Baker

*The Grimoire of Arthur Gauntlet* by David Rankine

*Thoth* by Lesley Jackson

*Thracian Magic* by Georgi Mishev

*Wicca Magickal Beginnings* by Sorita d'Este and David Rankine

www.ingramcontent.com/pod-product-compliance
Lightning Source LLC
Chambersburg PA
CBHW032009080426
42735CB00007B/551